Sonja Batinić-Besford was born in Belgrade (Yugoslavia),
with the Sun in Pisces, the Moon in Virgo and the
Ascendant in Scorpio. Sonja spoke fluently on her first
birthday, which she remembers well because the
celebration lasted for several days and she received many
presents, most memorably a little wooden chair and a red
handbag. Shortly after, she discovered the mysterious
beauty of life under the dining-room table covered with
a lace cloth full of trees and birds. Her world of listening
to the conversations above was interrupted only by her
grand-mother Ana passing down sandwiches. Sonja was
blissfully happy until (much earlier than usual, since her
parents considered her chosen life-style weird) she was
dispatched to school where she was very unhappy.
This lasted until, at the age of eight, she started to write:
reading and writing were natural extensions of her universe
under the table and all was well again.

Sonja has five books published in Belgrade, and many
short stories, poems and literary reviews in various
magazines in Britain, Yugoslavia, France and USA.
This, her third published collection of poetry,
is the first one written in English.

She is married to a dentist and lives in London.

GW00703530

*to john, always and forever*

# arrivals

*&*

# departures

∗

# sonja besford

*foreword by alan brownjohn*

*drawings by john besford*

*A S W A*

Published in 2001 by
The Association of Serbian Writers Abroad
PO Box 20772
London E3 5WF

ISBN 0-9541777-0-3

# contents

*foreword by alan brownjohn*  7

my mother my father  *15*
my mother my father II  *16*

meeting an aging prostitute  *21*
italian pimp  *23*
several sins  *24*
death of a friend in mombasa  *27*
the angel, the last prophet and death  *28*
photograph of a captured demon  *31*
devil and magician  *32*
the nun and the terrorist  *33*
to dance with bears and tigers  *35*
resentfully loving a prophet  *37*
goddess conducting rebirth  *38*
travelling with an angel  *39*
healer  *40*
homeless philosopher  *42*
the poet i know  *43*

dream lover  *46*
confession  *49*
tired love  *50*
tired love II  *51*
the virgin  *53*
lovers  *54*
waking with john  *57*
love poem  *58*

an affair  *59*

lust  *61*

abandoned dog  *62*

late love  *63*

alive again  *65*

the old man's temptation  *67*

return of the first lover  *68*

memories  *69*

the inner demons  *71*


februaring  *75*

serbs meeting luck  *77*

the tyranny of milošević  *78*

nato's 50th birthday party  *79*

serbia talking  *80*

troubled youth on his way to war  *83*

a mental patient  *85*

suicide of an actor in belgrade  *87*

a regime academic  *88*

hunger  *89*

the truth speaking  *91*

perhaps not a dream  *93*

singing  *95*

# Foreword

How do most readers approach collections of poetry?

Hardly ever, surely, reading from beginning to end, cover to cover, as we would with novels. Don't we first look at a couple of early poems to get a sense of what the author is doing, then move on and *select* other poems, either to read at once or leave until a little later, as decided by titles, opening lines, or length? And then don't we finally, to get some sense of what a book *as a whole* is saying, return and re-read it as a collection at that stage?

Poets know about these habits as readers; and are wise if they take some care about the first impression they offer, the last impression they leave, and the variety of subject, mood, size and shape in the poems placed between. It's a rare collection in which almost any poem you chance upon in this initially selective process of reading has the power – whether what it says is immediately clear or is more complex and requires a little more time – to hold the reader's attention at once.

Sonja Besford's poems in this vibrant and arresting book – I recommend looking immediately at, say, 'To Dance with Bears and Tigers' or 'Alive Again' – have just that ability. She writes with impressive command in a language not her mother tongue, which is Serbian, but refuses even to hint at the difficulties that task might present. It is almost as if the second language, English, is commanding *her*. Privately she speaks of Serbian as a 'wonderful husband' with whom she can feel too comfortable, and English as a 'vigorous young lover' driving her crazy with his 'passion, unpredictability, energy, originality and quite often delightful simplicity.'

Shall we take the husband first? Sonja began writing in English a few years ago with her reputation already well-established in her native Yugoslavia: she is the author of two poetry collections, two of short stories and a novel, all published in Belgrade. Reading the eight poems she has translated into English from the Serbian in part three of this book (they first appeared in her previous collections as well as the distinguished literary review *Kritika*), or those she has written in English, and wondering how they would read and sound in Serbian – as if we were the lover wondering about the husband, so to speak – it's possible to sense something of the surreal daring, the freedom to be *un*reasonable. That would excite English readers if they could also read her in her mother tongue. It's the same excitement they have felt about very much of the best post-Second World War poetry from Eastern Europe in general.

The English can write wonderfully in other ways – rationality is one of their hugest assets – but not in that particular way. So the comfortable husband remains a passionate rival? Yes, but the lover would be right to claim that there is something special and remarkable about Sonja's poems done in his English, to which she has brought abundant quantities of the verve and originality of her mother culture.

To begin where any reader will start: her gratitude to her parents is poignantly clear in the two introductory poems about them, tributes to their defiant, exuberant spirit ('they shiver yet sing') colourfully remembered in 'a ravelling of voices music cutlery napery', in the family Sunday lunches, the visits with her siblings to the cake shop and the cinema, and after the cowboy film

> ...our mother
> our father waiting to take us to our unhaunted home
> where even the walls sang and paintings hummed

The feeling of warmth and security caught there so vividly (that 'unhaunted' atmosphere) has given this poet the strength to take on an impressive range of themes; though it only intermittently returns in the poems that follow.

They are about: love, with its pleasures and ambiguities, time and memory – being young and growing old – good and evil, politics (which means, implicitly yet unmistakably, the plight of her mother country), and death. Aren't these the necessary stock-in-trade of most poets? True, but Sonja Besford specialises in a quality of unexpectedness which makes her variations of these traditional themes enthralling – and disconcerting. You do *not* know at once where you are in her poems, with the love poems in particular. Is 'Death of a Friend in Mombasa' a love poem? Is the speaker, wanting permission to let the tears flow, the poet? The sadness is patent, and the speaker will be unable to show a true face, only

> mourn...with the tragedy of a clown
> who has run out of the makeup removing cream

Love, which inevitably raises questions of time and memory, can be delighted in for its ability to disorientate the lover ('Love Poem'), doubted when the lover is just too grandiloquent (in the very funny 'An Affair'), or recalled with a kind of hopeful nostalgia ('Return of the First Lover'). It can be celebrated as a late happening ('Late Love'), or deeply ambiguous when, in 'Lust', the fascinated lovers feel 'poisoned by the lasting gift of lust', or exhausted and passing (in the two 'Tired Love' poems). Or tender and uncomplicated in marriage:

> i adjust to our curves and cavities, inhale
> his sleep-odours and so assembled by
> spoonfuls of love, every morning
> i wish it were yesterday morning
> ('Waking with John')

But no treatment of love, memory, or any other theme in these pages will be routine or conventional; the slant on 'Memories' in the poem of that title is both novel and entertaining. Unsurprisingly, there are intriguing and unusual ideas in those poems, often complex yet always rewarding, that examine good and evil. Some are written from a conviction that the Christian God will play a dangerous and deadly games with humanity, for example with the woman in 'Meeting an Aging Prostitute', who asks to be renewed so as to meet a first lover whom she *might* once have met beside 'an indigo lagoon' long ago. It is also possible that the lover never arrived and she became a prostitute, or, he made her into a prostitute. In any case the prayer is made in vain; so finally

> she calls out to her death-lord to lead her
> to the end and thence to the beginning and to that
> perfumed shore again

An alarming note of despair? In the cryptic, possibly very personal, poem called 'Resentfully Loving a Prophet', God withdraws immortality from someone and returns her to ordinary human existence to perform his will in respect of someone else. This is an uncertain universe…

This is a poet of arresting images and metaphors, but 'Healer' and 'The Inner Demons' are poems in which imagery sustains vigorous and challenging *argument*. In the latter poem, immense personal territories are covered, exuberantly and yet with the ruefulness that features so often in these pages. Can the demons be given last rites and laid to rest? It seems not. They can be annoyed, but not expelled, not ignored. The two people (lovers?), failing in their attempt to be rid of them, end up with an increased sense of their own awfulness ('what a melancholy / brothel we've become').

> in the texture of these ceremonies i felt my friend's
> goodness and lofty presence as we held hands
> to dance and leap towards the conciliatory moon lighting
> our faces and that graveyard in croatia i shall never see again

There has been a sort of wild enjoyment in this process of admitting their irreversible fallibility. And all this (not least the mysterious and sinister implications of the graveyard image) is achieved in just fourteen lines.

The reference to Croatia fittingly occurs in the last line before the Part TWO consisting of thirteen poems with a mainly political content. The mood is set, wittily, truthfully, and eloquently by the first, 'Februaring':

> i am februaring about all the dead friends and past lovers
> …who loved me without reconstructing me or devouring me,
> who enchanted my molecules and my senses and i am
>     februaring
> because there is much left to februar and it is, after all,
>     february

Sonja Besford deserves an Oxford English Dictionary entry for supplying a new verb 'to februar', to the English language; meaning 'simultaneously to remember, complain at, protest about, or even praise, aspects of life and/or nation in a spirit reflecting the climate of the month of February.' It is the most relaxed poem – and comprehensive, and extraordinary – in this political sequence, which otherwise mourns, in a fashion only Serbs can fully appreciate, the fate of her mother country in the late 1990s.

On the one hand there is (these are poem titles) 'The Tyranny of Milošević' and 'Regime Academic'; on the other 'NATO's 50th Birthday Party', a date celebrated by the infliction of death and suffering on a Yugoslavia which the West had rarely understood, had ceaselessly patronised, and was now intent on bombing and exploiting. 'A Mental Patient' (Belgrade During the Bombardment) also makes a point, clearly and forcefully. 'Serbia Talking' (first printed, like several other poems here, in the admirable London literary journal *Ambit*) is a poet's heartfelt manifesto about her country; which concludes

> that no true saviour is on his way, that my people are
> doomed and
> that all the whirling birds of prey have become killing
> machines

In 'The Truth Speaking', justice is powerless, but there is at least some hope that truth can 'glue itself together' again; a hope reinforced in 'Singing', the last poem of the collection, where the poet is saying that sadness about her country must be experienced so that it can be overcome by its 'essence', or spirit

> as if it were a nuisance louse and nothing more

In this book the poems come at the reader at a rush, without much punctuation, and in 'lower case' without capitals (except for the rare occurrence of the noun 'God'). It is a deliberate device, designed – the poet says privately – to symbolise 'personal humility of the "grain of sand" variety...I also cannot justify thinking of myself in capital "I" terms.' The effect is to enhance the passion of these strange, beautiful and humane poems, which – if I can try to rescue the phrase from the grasp of advertising – 'must be read', for what they say so grippingly about Sonja, Serbia and life in general; and the ways in which they say it. Her English readers are lucky to have this poet working so fruitfully – and movingly – in their language.

*Alan Brownjohn*

# my mother my father

how strange i thought how peculiar odd
they shiver yet sing: that's brave isn't it?
although life's mile end glimmers
on their finger nails and next
in my dream i saw them young
untouched unclaimed exquisite
sheltered by a sighted god
they sat on the earth floor singing away
the unforgiving trail of future tears while
the archons of darkness presented them
with a mystifying charmed dance but
my mother my father sang away their clench
their stench the vile smile of their sly promises

then i was born astonished
by their light godliness and loving commands
quick and tight like fearless midnight prayers
in a far away church and farther land
i listened to everything curved and filmy:
my mother knew music my father all the words
my mother felt plants my father all the animals
she celebrated st. john he st. nicholas
she drank vodka with lamb he brandy with pork
and all the while they sang and danced
a ravelling of voices music cutlery napery
in ever reducing circles
until they entered my heart's periphery
and marched in unstoppable

*First published in Ambit 156*

# my mother my father II

unexpectedly it was on hearing a mazurka
on one rainy-grey london day
that i remembered my mother my father
dancing in triple time to coppelia
skipping and sliding on a parquet floor
clicking heels and stamping feet;
listen to the **second** beat, mother exclaimed,
oh it's just not fast enough, father complained;
from all those years ago i see once more
my mother's radiant presence reflecting
her playful and dazzling haughtiness
wearing an orange hat tilted just so
towards her left eyebrow and red lips
ready to bewitch men and charm women;
i see my father with hunched shoulders holding
his hat against the whirling storm and icy wind
leaving the first footprints in the first snow
which squeaked creaked and squealed
like a happy dog after his master's affection;
i recall sunday lunches at the mercy of father's
pedagogy – today, girls, we shall discuss aristotle
or cicero or dostoyevski or the roman empire
or the economic strategies of imperialism —
or whatever, and we had to contribute, stealing
secret glances at the clock, wishing the time away (alas)
so that we could be released to run to the cake shop
with alluring odours of cream, nuts and chocolate,
for several *baklavas*, *tulumbas* and glasses of *boza*

(biljana would want one of everything
goga anything she could dismantle
i just watched
jasna wasn't born yet)
then to the cinema for the four o'clock performance,
three wide-eyed girls in flowery dresses licking ice-cream
while cowboys and indians hounded each other
in zane grey's formulaic brilliance and our mother
our father waiting to take us to our unhounded home
where even the walls sang and the paintings hummed

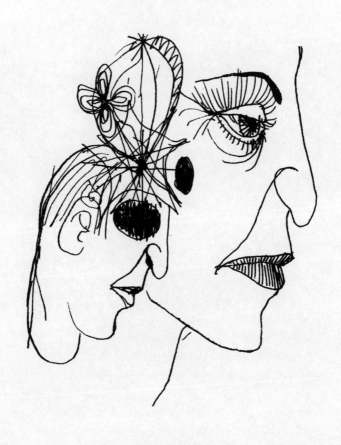

# meeting an aging prostitute

on her face and body freckles quarrel with
unmerciful creases etched by the heavy burden
of sold seductions, copulations and perversions
mostly unwelcome, mostly tedious, sometimes
repugnant; these days with increasingly long rests
between clients, behind her half-closed eyelids
grows a yearning for a far away landscape
she recalls leaving decades ago, perhaps imagined,
perhaps real, a vista of trees with heady scents of
jasmine, wisteria and lavender along an indigo
lagoon on whose shores she used to sit for hours
dazzled by peacocks' seductive dance displays and
dragonflies' iridescent mating whilst frequently
she could have been heard murmuring, if anyone
were near enough but no one ever was, an invitation
to her as yet unseen first lover to come through
the heat-shivering air towards her embrace and
her already opening sensuality;

after an age of dry waiting she knew it was the fickle
moods and treachery of her destinies which stopped him
appearing before her and so flamed by anger
she staggered into a world saturated with frightening
impurities and mutating sins – she arched to meet them all;

now, in the early evening as she sits on her spitalfields
bench, she keens a loud ode to the needle-rot spreading
in her body, then after midnight, exhausted and almost
unconscious, she calls out to her death-lord to lead her
to the end and thence to the beginning and to that
perfumed shore again

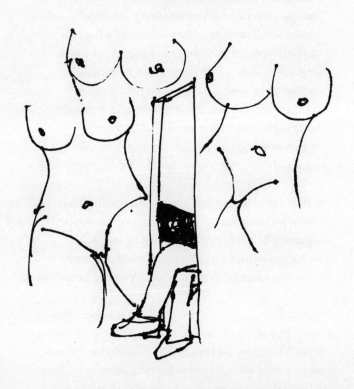

# italian pimp

in a hotel suite in nairobi he sits at his laptop,
emperor of bellies and breasts, mostly nocturnal
choreographer of shameless navels and nipples
because a noon light frequently scissors through
his complaining flesh with galloping pain down
along the amputated limb and prosthesis
as if a live leg, surprised at its own martyrdom
and stubbornness, continues to remind him of days
before his soul got shipwrecked on the oldest
rock of marshalling sin and slime

# several sins

it was by a fragrant cinnamon tree in the raw
mustiness of a tropical island which still
mourned capsized treasure-ships from
long ago that i noticed her at once:
turned towards the busy, foaming sea
she stood quite still her eyes distant
as if watching some now paling projection
full of brave pirates and other ghosts;
hidden behind a coconut palm my solitude
floated to embrace her grave beauty
to own and take her like a love-sick beast
then to rummage through her goodness and
filter out the many poisons from my soul;
but before i could make her my remedy
a handsome man suddenly appeared and like
some professional, daring and tactile god
his hands instantly journeyed over her body
his lips kissed her neck whispering hot
words in love-tongues i have never known
i have never been taught to know
his body urgently pressed against hers
like a capricious ivy in a glutinous race
to hypnotise, enter and fill a virgin wall;
that cayenne anger of mine immediately roared
in the panting tune with the howling envy until
my ears were two demented, jealous drums
screaming vengeance at her easy consent
to his rogue ways to possess and dissemble
her innocent beauty and milky chastity;

then came lust for her responding passion
followed by another fury at my own impotence
to make her love transfer from him to me
so that i am no longer an unremarkable
accurately named atlas of human frailties,
an unremembered mass heading for oblivion
but rather a man loved by her:
a hero

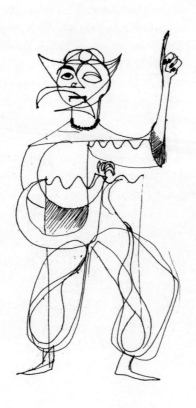

*First published in Kritika*

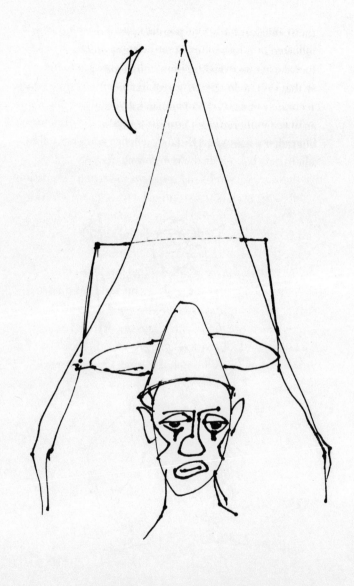

death of a friend in Mombasa

# death of a friend in mombasa

in my mind, it is the final picture of his golden body
still and flickering in the semi-darkness under
a crescent moon, stars and a candle-lit mosquito net
which haunts me over and over like a never-ending lament
it retraces its journey until at dusk my head servant comes in
with iced white wine and my dogs bark in the distance
chasing the sea foam lighted by jellyfish and dragonflies
while fruit-bats circle the ylang-ylang trees —
all these are just emblems and signs towards a permission
to close my eyelids at last and to let tears slip
to my upper lip and to a waiting tongue;
much later in the lonely tedium of the humid night
i trace the staccato lanes of my memories
divine at their source as only eternal love must be
from the moment we met walking the sands of shanzu
to the heat of his breath against my hairline as he
guided me through the samba and out of despair —
oh i mourn for him with the tragedy of a clown
who has run out of the make-up removing cream

# the angel, the last prophet and death

it was an indelicate Godly fantasy
— i must never speak of it again —
which lent me to your world and wrapped me
into this conspiracy of yours and His
to embrace and then possess the last cross —
obeying my true Saviour's will
i painted your nails with gold dust
your skin with lavender oils to lust
after my sabre-brain and willing body
i danced for you on burning coals
keeping time with your slow pulse —
and with the captivated kneeling crowds
i too revered your glowing divinity
the holy aura and the haunting eloquence
later to voyage you over my body
courageous tempestuous on and on
until on a chill morning of sad omen
i climbed the ylang-ylang tree
to solace with my seven herons —
and saw her at once glimmering on the dunes
a beautiful apparition of urgent calamities
crowned with oleander and mimosa
skirted with silks and tinkling pearls
her eyes struggling to contain her chaos
shone dissembling love to yours

which silently widened with wonder —
your hands shook your hips trembled
your tired ribs opened to let her enter
at last – and i did not lament as i long to
but like the just born eighth heron
i flew and flew and flew singing thunderstorms
my new wings imprisoning your dying scent

*First published in Ambit 156*

# photograph of a captured demon

i was open vulnerable and just ready to convert her
when a strange sound and bursting light distracted me
so that ever since i have been stuck in an album on a
photograph showing the face of a nun in a virtuous prayer
and behind her my shadow in a spasm of lust for her
virginal moans and the scent from her damp thighs;
my captured form now weeps when it remembers
millenniums of classic conquests, i, trophy-hunter of the
chastities of nuns monks maidens grammar school kids
who eagerly accepted my offer of lasting bondage
to the stirrings of their dangerous libidos;
now flattened nostalgic and vexed i ravish only in my
paling memories and only when the volume is opened
during the episodic visitations by acid-taking
glue-sniffing teenagers in the basement of a hospital
where a single boiler bulb lights a photograph and
duplicates the images of body parts from old x-rays
scattered on the concrete floor and from there
i see her as well old and dying in a ward upstairs
still believing that she was photographed with
the shadow of an angel behind her

*First published in Ambit 166*

# devil and magician

tonight you retreated into the darkened room
again not missing the cat killing ceremony
the drinking of blood and the foaming dance
over the transfiguration of my body —
long after, your scent hazed over the wine
the silk sheets and my painted erotic bruises —
i laughed swaying behind your left shoulder
oh what a magical conjurer you might have been
had i not seduced you into believing in the only great
scheme, immortality, and now in anticipation of it
your life flickers into an indulgent migraine

# the nun and the terrorist

perhaps it was a verbal tradition within our elders'
immutable decrees which made me offer him shelter
in our mission with its nomadic memories its scrolls
and old ghosts who wished him frosty welcome and
speedy farewell while i gave him a pearly rosary and
a chalice with a cure for his infectious sadness
his frequent tears and facial paralysis;
many a night i held him in my still strong ancient arms
singing him into dreams of his murderous recollections
then banishing his screams and howls to our tolerant
mangroves with only one entrance and no way out;
often after listening to his memories of slaying
i would rush out to the nymphs to dance on the moaning
magma blistering my skin and charring my nails
hoping that i would draw off his deadly venom and he
would shine once again with his now dormant goodness;
and then on one earthly morning when i saw nothing
in his eyes but a frenzied need to kill again and leave
this weary place of failing absolution i told him to follow
the river and journey out through the mangroves

## to dance with bears and tigers

he said that he would guide me through
the remote memories of lives i had forgotten
to collect at the entrance to this one;
he suggested that my family should be ignored
for they are only transiting tenants in a heritage-
cemetery invented by destinies cheated of physical
substance and always ready to seek revenge;
he caressed me into an exquisite trance to dance
again with bears and tigers on a glowing meadow
to ride on a comet's tail to swim in a sun-spot
to visit the dark side of the moon
to know all answers to all riddles
and now so enriched i drift trying in vain
to remember **more** while he is slowly disinfecting
his love for me and exhausted by my remoteness
he wishes to leave but still cannot
being so raptured by my dance with bears and tigers
who remember me with panting lust from their past
human life when we were all scented with musk and
rosemary oil in the house of mirrors and shaded lights
and multiplied sighs

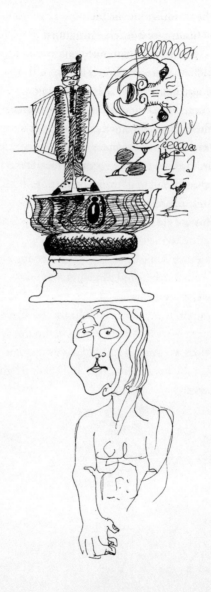

# resentfully loving a prophet

so now it is the beautiful you who knows
how to disanchor me how to sail me in tune
with your mysterious incantations hypnotic
sacraments et cetera while i chant and tie
indignant knots around crystals and talismans
of depleted power that i inherited from a loving
greek hermaphrodite centuries ago when people
built **me** shrines to pray to **my** incandescent
omnipotence: i stopped floods earthquakes
avalanches i burst hail-clouds lifted caribbean
hurricanes buried sahara sand-storms —
this was all routine shit believe me;
and now just look at me: i am contaminated
by human mortality which is meant only
to guard guide and love your immortality

# goddess conducting rebirth

in the venerable glow of the african moon
i watched an old man being reborn
his skin was lined his nails were worn
as he unpicked his past lives from a loom
which twirled skipped sang and mingled
with buzzing mosquitoes and flying fox bats
until singing high up to my thirteen blind cats
i made up his future from the first cell singled
and in the womb it grew to a rosy child
then to emerge into a new life with an old scream
filing a rich claim that life is an ancestral dream
held in my many heads some wise some wild

# travelling with an angel

he clings to the angel's shoulders not understanding
the purpose of this long flight or the world below's
obsession with macabre games and tragic ends
from needless mastectomies to mass suicides
from rented affections to sacrificial prayers —
but he does fathom love and the rumours that it
always wins unless it's starved by negligent fools
even before impotence or lack of desire takes over —
from time to time he tries to shout a question:
it bounces off the clouds and cosmic junk
to disappear into the angel's deaf left ear

*First published in Ambit 166*

# healer

you certainly are a healer and a mighty poison for every
metastasis of shame and pain as well as a convertible
medicament against the bleeding gums and the stinking
odour of garlic and wine;
you smell of sea-salt, cinnamon, vanilla, peppermint,
of recent kisses, burning thighs, pleasurable undulations
in the lower stomach;
you cure ancient misfortunes, spasms, paralyses, wrongly
glued genes and hesitant palms with a mixture of mandrake,
butter, dead nettles;
you heal the lame with hot chestnuts on their chests and greasy
soot on the last vertebra then above it and below it, and sideways
on and on until they stand up and walk, although i suspect that
your lymph glands are always plotting a parabolic curve ending
in the immediate ingestion of the cured spirit;
if an admiring researcher would rip open the glands, all your
caressed mistresses-believers, followers, adorers, prudent
sisters, adopted mothers, merciful daughters, would
leap out to whisper:
each one of your sugar-laced words is meant only for me,
my love you love, my aspects you recognise, my senses
you sense;

then: immigrants, impetuous exhibitionists, hidden perverts,
drugged doctors, inventive revolutionaries, would also jump
out to maintain that each one of your sugar-laced words is meant
only for him, his love you love, his aspects you recognise, his
senses you sense, and all the while you seldom laugh, as you used
to long ago with that spiced woman from the ruins of belgrade,
under the morning mist above the rivers' confluence and her skin
on yours, because for eternity now in between the abused earth
and unnamed heavens, you are discovering nothing in
everything, although many believe that in between the unabused
earth and the named heavens,
you are illuminating all in everything, but it seems, yes, it does
seem that i am still too salty, too far away and now you can no
longer reach me to keep me

# homeless philosopher

outwardly dangerous he hides his gloom
by posing at the foothills of many solitudes
together with charcoal-burners and beggars
who wear wilted roses behind each ear and
an embroidered left shirt cufflink as if to smirk
at the suffocating grief which defines this world
of life and atones the adjacent one of death
or was it the other way around

# the poet i know

in his acidic words he celebrates
the future of humanity within a world
he paints as lunatic and negligent
clumsy from promises no one cares to keep
as if reasoning and truth surgically implanted
at the embryonic stage were then bandaged with lies,
those fat ambitious parasites who feed on our will
as flies do on excrement

# dream lover

it's been a long tide of many springs since i could vividly recall your lovely face, your tempting body and two-tongued words caressing my ego and waking my lust with piercing aim and messianic grace; it has been a long slide of many summers since you spooked my love-making with later lovers circling above my memories of us together like a bird of prey searching out a moving meal then stooping and settling down between me and any man mocking all the usual courtesies which most of my partners inclined to bestow who saw me as czarina at the table and in bed; but like a true diviner, you could see at once, couldn't you, that i was indeed a czarina at the table but a wanton whore in bed: speedily, confidently you subpoenaed my catacombs of harlot-treasures, prised them open without my permission or consent, tossed them and whipped them into a fanatical lust for you until nothing else mattered: my heart was bruised, my rosary broken, my gods denounced, my friends forgotten; frantic like a crippled creature crazed from pain, i eloped with despair as my captive companion – ran, hid, ran further and on to a cloister of the damned whose lives were sunk by shadowy masters too and thence to this refuge where nothing disturbed my preferred idea that you were just an imagined impostor and dream-crusher who barged into my foggy reality for no reason but to have fun;

now after all this effort i've spent in forgetting you and us – not touching anyone not wanting to be the woman you knew – you stand at my sanctuary's gates in all your still glorious beauty like some ex-emperor reminding his ex-mistresses and wives that his empire and rule must never be forgotten: you arrogantly demand that i stop pushing my life away from yours because (you say) my heart can never expel its love for you or reverse your long past steep descent into my lasting passion; you further profess to love and want me even more than before, more than the finest poets and troubadours gave witness as if your years-long journey to find me confirmed it like the journey deserved me but does it really – without speaking and on a trembling step i turn aside to close and lock these forbidding doors all over again to continue a dream without the physical you and i know there'll be many long autumns and many long winters till i stop remembering the real you and for the last time it will be when the moon stumbles and my stars fade away

# confession

he has no one not even me to blame for
the secrets he told me that autumn afternoon
when he forgot my identity my past and present
after we had drunk two bottles of white wine
eaten smoked salmon followed by some other
non-scavenging fish (we were at bloom's)
all the time stripteasing his brain of memories
all the time reviewing past carnal flings until he said:
frankly i always believed any international fuck,
even an eu fuck (we laughed for a moment) was
preferable to falling in love with a real woman
or so i thought three years ago;
at first she was no one
then a riot of senses which sliced me with desire;
she gave herself to me in instalments then absolutely
and became an irresistible hook to my rental amnesia
eager to forget my wife my children my friends:
i crippled then murdered my inner warnings and reason —
he stopped and stared at his upturned palms
calling back those lighted days before she left him
while i sat swallowing screams and regrets about his
migrating heart for i knew well his wife and children
and remember well the days of no laughter three years
ago – we didn't say much after that and since
my husband and i

# tired love

oblivious to the vultures who circle
ominously yet gracing the faultless sunset
you rage at the pink-veined marble carving
the body-shape i used to have
before i grew fat on wine and tears
blotchy with age and bitter fears
born long ago by that sinister force
which roams the tired olive groves of umbria
when stunned by love and ecstasy
you wept and called my name
to be answered by that malign entity
which searches out the in-love lame —
oh if only we had our eyes closed
our bodies covered and protected
by more than just each other's —
since then you have angrily elected
to close all benign memory shutters:
why why are you so eager to sign us off
to let us have so much and yet be not

*first published in Ambit 156*

# tired love II

you journey to hurt me as naturally as tears obey
gravity tracking to my cheek lips tongue and neck,
a salty ambush for my not so hidden purity
which loves you less and less —
long ago in florence, in the lit gardens of villa cora
one terraced stranger told me:
all truths are hidden in the inkspots and the chandeliers,
they confirm there is no **good** god, i know, i used to be
his confessor, he finished in whisper;
believing him mad and blasphemous, i ran from fear
into your chaos and your plot to improve every
aspect of my personality – then suddenly it was too late;
now you say that i embarrass you and i, moonless with shame,
grow colder and set not unlike chilled lava: brittle
    and full of holes —
oh i used to be so good at loving and loving you especially

# the virgin

he commanded me to love him
to compass my novice sensuality
towards his capricious mind and senses
jazzled by jimsonweed and alkaloids —
he flew high higher to and beyond lunacy
bathed in his marinade with full or absent grace —
he commanded me to love him and i did
love him for a long long while until
he wanted me to jump down a whole mile

# lovers

we decided to meet at heathrow's cargo section
among the sentient murmur of customs officers
fluent in detection of counterfeit and drugs
i didn't know him, this ljubomir, a man from my land
a friend of a friend and first cousin of another,
this ljubomir whose name means lover of peace
who arrived with his black piano for no other would do
on his concert tour through these islands' patchy welcomes

long ago when i was a boy and he a young man
i heard him play one august night just before we sailed
from dubrovnik to bari, and all the magic music through
with closed eyes i strained to lock him in my head
within my nurtured dream of priestly solitude
but as years marched and died his image found an easy exit
or perhaps i cleared it out to make space for many a lonely other
sometimes less deserving but more in need of a brother

now he stood here grey-haired, dressed in a black suit
a motionless defender of his black piano and his music sheets
unused to and perplexed by the customs officers' courtesies
i hurried to him, shook his hand, even bowed a little
then reached to embrace him as we slavs often do
when his summer breath behind my ear unlatched my senses —
surprised, we gasped and blushing sprang apart exposed
to stumble out, i awkwardly polishing my lenses

i remember something of what happened through that day
we talked i know and laughed a lot and choked
on food and wine when our knees touched under the table —
mindful of slav laws, our protocol and codes

we wasted time with recollections, walked in town
before crashing with each other in the dusky zones
focussed on unfurling everything gentle and cruel
every active, hungry cell and every shameless rule


and to ljubomir i say

you loved me fiercely then serenely then violently again
you shattered my shyness by intoning mesmerising notes
and recomposed my essence each time more divine
less fragile more alluring more immortal in design
as i restored your faded fantasies and distant dreams
uninhibited and mischievous we blazed throughout the night
like a fire in a heatwave burning with a sinful might
until nothing was any longer entirely yours or entirely mine

now so i hear you play the world like no other
weaving that single night-long love into yearning songs
hundreds of admirers, disciples, mistresses light your way
across the latitudes and longitudes of many nation's borders
where you have nothing to declare but this silent prayer
for a female reflection of me and i remain eminent, elegant
in my exiled invisibility, silent in pain and unaccountable
for i am the keeper of many secrets and you are the loveliest of all

*First published in Kritika*

# waking with john

always at dawn i wake-up
to a blackbird singing and wait
listening to his breathing and wait
for his senses to open to mine and wait
for his body to turn, his eyes to open
and wait for his laughter to say:
you look like a lioness ready to pounce
which i do, masterfully covering his torso
with one swift, unhesitant move
i adjust to our curves and cavities, inhale
his sleep-odours and so assembled by
spoonsful of love, every morning
i wish it were yesterday morning

*First published in Kritika*

# love poem

sometimes quite unexpectedly i inhale
his aroma in the foreign blades of cut grass
for instance in a park in boston or among
the cinnamon trees in the brief garden in
sri lanka: there i could even taste his salt
in the remembered tantrum of my fingers
which, just as he taught me, knew well
how to move through our moist love making
dissolving shyness and regrets;
yes, it happens quite often that i measure my own
life with the weight and length of the dreams
he braided for me in his parallel reality
until i could no longer find peace or myself

## an affair

you say that "our illicit liaison
presents a hypnotic conjugation
of two nomadic bodies exhausted
by their impious journeys through
bestial curiosities over transient skins"—
furthermore that "those distant events are
now mouldy nodules of sheer nothingness
so far beneath my glowing sanctuary"—
but
when you go home and i remain alone
accompanied only by your grandiloquence
in my head, i wonder with invading fear whether
i am the receptacle of your well oiled lies
or your staggered-upon true love

# lust

after he handed her the ceremonial chalice
to drink a sticky liquid in worship of his gods
and discover which animal would choose her
speak through her and make her dance a dream,
his ravishing perfumed beauty embraced her,
his fingers the owners of ancient crafts and motions
chimed over her skin, ringing the wake-up call—
she moved, now following him, now leading him
both elegant like green mambas in a baobab tree
descending and climbing, their bodies making
s-shaped loops to lurch forwards and backwards
and sideways all according to the reptiles' so slow
oh – so – so slow evolutionary etiquette;
they welcomed the gateway to this adulterous night
and rode on the unregretted mercy of it until
the miracle of a new day shimmered in the mirrors
and they parted, he to his mountains, she to her
flatlands, across the ocean, beyond guilt but both
poisoned by the lasting gift of lust

# abandoned dog

it is too late to start denouncing him now
that man who some years ago still spoke
with an innocent tongue i understood well
who drew paintings in the wine caves of the rhone
while i, clean and loved, barked merrily
startling bats and owls into an early jig;
it is too late to start regretting my fragile friendship
with a traitor in disguise who left me
as soon as i had shed too many hairs and tumours
had begun to gallop through my veins —
now as the malignant swellings press against my skull
filthy and unloved, i embrace all my sweet memories
and the last fragrance of his hand upon my head

# late love

this is so unusual for me
for all this life i walked on nettles
learnt how to kiss
young men's hands and temples
learnt how not to miss
subtle signs of turmoil or despair
how to make them light and
soar with pride as they achieve
such might such heady height —
so kind so full of sight you praise me
and older than my father would have been
you wish me to believe you and receive you
as if i were the innocent clean tongued maiden
and you as pure as the first ocean's swell
oh how unusual this is for me
almost like entering my own death again

*First published in Kritika*

# alive again

at the start of the rancid state of aging
i've read all the signs accurately and seen
that there's no one to blame or persecute
no one to scream at or plead to for a return
journey ticket to the glorious years
before dementia and life-eclipse started
hissing at the entrance to each ear;
it seemed that nothing bright could happen
to reverse or undo this deliberate dying
this enchantment with fading memories
until one walk she emerged into the sunlight
in front of a just born rainbow, so free
so divinely mobile under a huge yellow umbrella
shinning and glittering as if dipped in pure gold
her breasts pointing to the celestial heights
oh, i regained my horns again and hoarsely
like any old renegade i whispered to her
that i was mistaken and not dead after all —
she smiled and set her lips on mine
her tongue thrusting my death further
to a distant waiting room and that night
i was a pilgrim, a mariner, a rich man, a beggar
and she a virgin, my tender love, my whore
and that night we needed nowhere to run
nowhere to sail nowhere to fly or land
but on to each others' skin and psyche
and that night i got hold of my life again

# the old man's temptation

she was sitting exactly opposite me
from mile end to queensway reading
my book on how successfully to conceal
the major signs of age by converting
bad conquests into invented kissing tales
(almost at the entrance to bragging)
about all the passing females and males
who boasted almost nothing sagging
and whose desire for every reader always wins
in order to visit a multitude of our secret sins —
then suddenly i had the strangest need
a temptation to place my lips on her knee
only god knows where it may slowly lead
even perhaps on to her iliac crest's lee
and so on that ridge i can travel in style
her fragrant beauty lighting my last mile
but sadly that day i was far too old and meek
and she too young to know why & what i seek —
we parted without even a goodbye look
her fingers still clutching my wise book
mine inventing one wholly new patella story
full of forbidden joy and unexpected glory

*First published in Ambit 166*

# return of the first lover

it isn't strange (why should any repetition ever be)
how fast again your inner shadow recognised mine
both fragmenting and melting in foreign embraces
which deny the remote significance of dried blood
upon the young hunger of our thighs and stomachs;
it isn't strange (why should any distant memory ever be)
for long ago i have seen you lit by your mother's light
and i can read your love poems in the half circle of your
cut off cuticles now lying on a tissue ready to be burnt
so that neither i nor any powerful one can cast a spell
to make you fall out of love with me – again
and even for a while

# memories

i have a hidden suitcase packed with misadventures
foggy judgments and random decisions as well as
such beauty, such celebrations of life, such loves
that when i open the lid a miasma rich with honey,
sea and pines hazes out purifying and embracing me
like an insomniac alchemist of long ago
nourished by his own power and cunning tongue
who took me to the dunes of malmo to dismantle my
tormented memories to dissolve them with rose
oils while ravens sermoned to the first light

# the inner demons

that summer i suggested that we should conduct
the last rights for our inner demons
(with full religious service and a brass-band) and
he being a choleric artist insisted on bread, sea salt
and red wine just to annoy these all powerful spirits
we knew we could never kill or expel or ignore
— they would stay as long as they pleased —
what a funeral farce, we laughed and what a melancholy
brothel we've become, filled with genetic calamities
howling for our blood and for particles of forgiveness —
yet in the texture of those ceremonies i felt my friend's
goodness and lofty presence as we held hands
to dance and leap towards the conciliatory moon lighting
our faces and that graveyard in croatia i shall never see again

# februaring

i am februaring, captured by an annual ascending melancholy
eyes above my earthbound life, my soul at half-mast
in slow orbit around recollections and regrets:
i am remembering all my teachers who tried to mould me
with linguistic storms, mystifying metaphors and even spells
into a more ordinary native or at least a less eccentric exile;
i am remembering all my friends who tried to nourish me
with sweet injections of vanity and luminous flattery which
promised to glue my ever fragmented brain into an entirety;
i am remembering the sadness of my far away homeland
full of weeping women, refugees, orphans and hungry innocents
whose destinies were as chiselled by some bitter frosty god,
by bloodthirsty warriors, politicians and journalists, so that
no land is safe, no land is safe, especially not mine;
i am februaring about all the dead friends and past lovers
who healed my wounds with laughter-potions and love-
     ointments
who abstained from being tourists (in this life and any other)
who loved me without reconstructing me or devouring me,
who enchanted my molecules and my senses and i am
     februaring
because there is much left to februar and it is, after all, february

# serbs meeting luck

we approached her from the side
she smelt of soap and something round;
we had no music and no voice then or now
so we tapped her thyroid gland:
come, please be ours;
i have never been anyone's here,
she drew the letters on our palms and left
at four that afternoon, ten years ago

*First published in Kritika, translated from Serbian by SB & JB*

# the tyranny of milošević

there is a musty corrupt dominion
whose subjects drift on a shrinking slave ship
hidden in a paralysing fog of fears
moidered by swinging lies and sneers
bedevilled by the evil rapacious criminal
his slayers, servants and their endless time

*First published in Kritika, translated from Serbian by SB & JB*

# nato's 50th birthday party

"doing nothing is not an option"

this is the phoney rage of the mighty with
hooligan brains which embraces hades
to ravage my people poisoning killing
maiming them pushing them into oblivion
from high above and far away
not caring how many deaths grace this bloody
march april may june july forever as long
as it is a good exercise for nato, said clinton
followed by blair's mad stare babbling from his eyes
and confirmed by their bloodthirsty rhetoric of
cluster bombs and depleted uranium

*First published in Kritika*

that night as the lunar rainbow crossed my vulnerable skies and hawks led flocks of vultures to circle in the hot sirocco swirls, ignoring all hazards, i stopped casting spells, making ancient sacrifices and praying to the divine ears of a moody God; instead, i lifted my essence to the highest tower to scan the spread mountains, the valleys, rivers and lakes: hourly i hoped that my old predictions would come true, so that the lazy, shimmering horizon would conjure up a tall mast, then swollen sails above a white ship on whose helm i would see the arriving saviours who would bring us harmony peace prosperity and to me a love to make all other loves i have had embarrassed with their comparative insignificance;

i became the gentleness of that night, framed by the scent of burning wood, salt air and the distant hot desert storms; i ignored the impatient flapping of wings all around me thinking that this time no bird of prey would harm me because for the first time tonight, just as i had wished for years, i turned over the four of wands as the tarot card of the future before me: it reads – even when reversed – harmony, peace, prosperity and great love;

the rainbow danced a slanting dance in the waveless lake-waters, the stars sparkled randomly, the birds cast ominous shadows, which i continued to ignore, and visions started to open before me just as, i supposed, life and death would open, if the evil king of my land had not quarantined them both almost immediately after he seized power; and, because life and death are identical twins and confined together, no one ever knows who among my people is alive and who is dead or indeed whether they exist as people at all; the scientists say that people are far too content with tacitly tip-toeing around this uncertainty; the artists claim that people are far too dulled by the felicity of the life/death state which requires no striving but yet sustains fears; the philosophers maintain that this seemingly unsolvable puzzle comprises the maxima of each individual and thus our people are always brave and triumphant to which i often reply that all three views are possible although only those who **solve** the puzzle will be victorious and never those who **merely define** it; the three groups are unimpressed by my answer (frankly, so am i) and probably expect much more from an oracle who sixteen centuries ago led her people to this mysterious, exquisite land to become its mother-earth, fertile from her people's blood and sacrifice:

i am serbia, the sum of all my people, the sum of their memories, their dreams, histories, wars, their defeats and victories;

i often visit the twins in their geometrically weird crystal prison, touch their transparent, margaric furniture, and see everywhere, below, above, all around, the moving images of the life and death forces guiding earthly forms into their allocated positions and i wonder whether the beautiful twins originally manoeuvred me too towards their future prison so as to fulfil some kind of meaningful prophecy, something instrumental to them and the whole of humanity, but i can never persuade them to admit to anything; they smile benignly at me, attentive and gentle, eager to discuss almost any topic i choose, they are childishly delighted when they make me laugh and please my curiosity, they sing and dance for me but they always manage to avoid my clever (and not so clever) verbal traps designed to reveal which one is life and which one is death;

they applauded when i told them that at last i had turned up the four of wands and they whirled me around holding hands, laughing, singing and exclaiming how especially dazzling i looked at that moment and how from the beginning of times there had never been a more beautiful, more proud, more brave and more dear to them female-oracle, mother-earth, the sum of her people and how, when the saviours arrive i must ask them to cast a lure, but why, i asked perplexed, why would a sailor know how to cast a lure, isn't falconry something that desert and mountain men are good at?, precisely!, they answered in unison and i could immediately see that they would tell me nothing further;

now as i stand here on the top of our world, staring into a darkened horizon, their request still seems odd, obscure; i turn around and see them in their quarantined glass chambers, gazing at me and at once the very centre of me shivers and contracts in a spasm of recognition: both life and death are blazing at me a quantity of love i have never seen before and i realise that i also love them with equal force; all at once i see that they came to me because i, serbia, and i alone am able to contain that amount of love, to belong to life and death equally, to please life and death equally, to offer them my body, my soul, my children, my sorcery, my four of wands equally, to be their muse and lover and they my mentors and lovers; they extend their arms beckoning me and i run towards them not turning back although i hear the sirens, the exploding bombs, while the king's and the saviours' laughter is so loud that i cannot hear the sum of my own screams and i know that no true saviour is on his way, that my people are doomed and that all the whirling birds of prey have become killing machines

*First published in Ambit 157*

## troubled youth on his way to war

who is this innocent actor of bravery
not long ago during his childhood
in a preface to his short-necked night
he grafted love and hope onto a zebra crossing
to a fertile field of books and music and now,
look, it is all burnt, mute and dead, does anyone care
whether his life is flying or he is holding on to it
with his little finger round the fast approaching epilogue

*First published in Kritika, translated from Serbian by SB & JB*

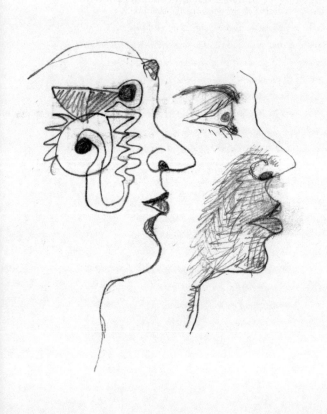

# a mental patient
## (belgrade during the 1999 bombardment)

i was breathing quietly, kneeling and trembling in what used to be
a white shirt, beyond the metal bars in a soft room with no windows;
the four eyed healer was knitting clever explanations:
we're out of medication, it follows that you're more powerful;
he wouldn't believe that i'm not, although i could follow his logic;
long ago i bartered my suit for a cup of blood from a reliable vampire;
from my first rib he aspirated a magical spell: it didn't work;
today the four-eyed healer left my door open, intentionally i suspect;
i hobbled to the attic, mother slept all curled up and cold;
this is the way, go to the roof, said another healer and in english!
i'd forgotten how good i used to be at all those mighty languages
(six to be precise, not including latin or church slavonic, naturally);
okay, okay, good for us, what? skip over the hair?, great!,
fly, fly with the bombs! i shouted sooo amused;
hang on to the cluster bomb! he ordered; they're like silver-coated
rain drops, which one shall i choose? i asked, counting aloud:
cinquanta, sessanta, settanta, ottanta, novanta, cento, duecento!
be quiet and don't you dare let go or i'll screw your... he threatened;
oh, i shan't, i shan't, i answered merrily, i shan't... secretly sniggering
at the moron-healer who hadn't worked out that i have been screwed
every way and everywhere by saints and sinners, by gods and devils
since i was born and probably well well before;
the bomb and i are flying, i inhale particles of depleted uranium, divine!,
mother still sleeps all curled up and cold and vampire-doctors sleep and
murderer-politicians sleep, pilots and arms-dealers sleep, journalists sleep,
but at last further buried i am no longer mortally awake and alone

*First published in Kritika, translated from Serbian by SB & JB*

# suicide of an actor in belgrade

first he ate his nails, then his left arm up to the elbow;
on the seventh day at dawn, instead of a ticket he offered
the conductor his tape-worm, pink, alive, in a glass-jar;
this is all i have, he said to the gaping mouth before he
jumped on the next track meeting the express train

*First published in Kritika, translated from Serbian by SB & JB*

# a regime academic

i polish the soiled shoes of my tamed steps: through
inherited pupils of fear i see my purgatory, oily, cruel, fated —
i fear darkness, insubordinate women, lascivious lips, thighs
alongside my adam's apple;
i'm afraid to flow into the powerful essences of unguessable
female seesaws – they wish to change me, stroke me, mother me,
love me, adopt me, cut loose my inner terrors;
i fear the ashtray of cigarette ends and the empty wine glasses
after immodest confessions;
i'm afraid of happiness, unhappiness, laughter, television:
it films me, it listens to me;
a book reads me, verses drain me into a stinking sweat;
i'm terrified in a lift, on a pedestrian crossing;
i fear someone replaying and shouting, so i do not speak
against or for anything or anyone;
quietly i open always side entrances while from my chest
i wipe my future ashes with a trembling handkerchief;
almost invisible, almost dead, i am a stranger everywhere,
in hiding

*First published in Kritika, translated from Serbian by SB & JB*

# hunger

in the basement grows a fatless mirror
it ripples odours of rotten onions
mouldy potatoes on the floor —
above, in his bed, a rat
smokes a cigar, drinks

*First published in Kritika, translated from Serbian by SB & JB*

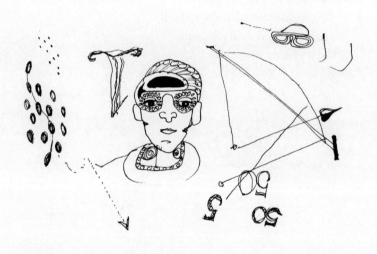

# the truth speaking

i was in a tired orchard
dozing under a parasol
when justice came to pay homage
to my earth-old human captors —
it left them unmarked, still lying,
although now stinking of death;
later, in my secret chambers,
the divided parts of me were partly
assembled and soon i shall glue
them into my entirety again

*First published in Kritika, translated from Serbian by SB & JB*

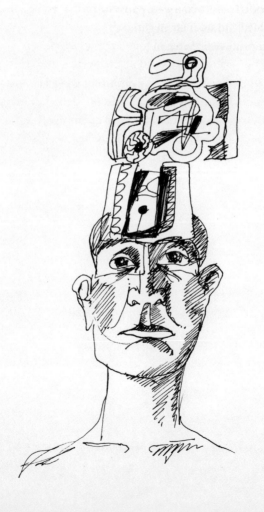

# perhaps not a dream

in my dream i saw a bazaar where merchants sold
men-assassins, killer wolves and venomous snakes,
where post-experimental corpses were fed to human
cripples and they when fat to privileged foreign visitors
who shared the hobby of poisoning children and watching
them die: slowly —
between these sessions, on seats made from dead infants' skins,
the guests sat on a roller-coaster being further entertained
by constant virgins high on survival;
in the same dream i listened to a dazzling sermon on
natural laws natural truths and natural justice
delivered by somehow familiar fornicator and a liar
followed by another dispenser of falsehoods and death —
so harmed i woke in tears to see them on my television
screen an evil nebula flickering behind their heads

*First published in Kritika*

# singing

please do not sing or hum at my funeral
for my people and i are not used to honouring
death with melodious notes but would
rather prefer to cry our sorrows and regrets
oh for so many things we failed to do and say
when we could have spoken with golden tongues
and unknotted hearts about naming the forms of love
for each other or singing sweet songs to please
us, the ears of gods and make angels dance;
please do not sing or dance at my funeral
for i should like to feel from not so far above
your sadness spread to enter your blood stream
to travel through your body to the skull and hair
then, my essence will descend and it shall comb it out
as if it were a nuisance louse and nothing more

*First published in Kritika*

designed by john morgan
typeset in bulmer monotype
cover designed by john besford
printed by the cromwell press, wiltshire
on 90gsm antique wove